THE RAMBAM

THE RAMBAM

A Brief Biography

•

Published by

MERKOS L'INYONEI CHINUCH
770 Eastern Parkway
Brooklyn, New York 11213

5745 — 1985

PHOTOCOMPOSITION BY

EMPIRE PRESS

550 EMPIRE BLVD. • BROOKLYN, N. Y.

Bookmart Press, Inc.
N. Bergen, N.J. 07047

TABLE OF CONTENTS

PREFACE

This biography is being published as tens of thousands of Jews in communities all over the world prepare to mark, on the day before Passover, the 850th birthday of Rabbi Moshe ben Maimon, universally known as Rambam, or Maimonides, with the completion of a year's study of his voluminous magnum opus "Mishneh Torah."

About one year ago, in a public address during Passover 5744/1984, the Lubavitcher Rebbe, Rabbi Menachem M. Schneerson שליט"א, proposed that everyone study and complete during the course of one year Rambam's entire "Mishneh Torah." For those who found this pace too difficult the Rebbe suggested that they complete this study in a three year cycle, or, as a third option, to study and complete in one year Rambam's "Sefer HaMitzvot."

The call by the Rebbe evoked an overwhelming response from Jews all over the world and tens of thousands have followed the schedule of study ever since.

As the response to the Rebbe's suggestion grew it triggered renewed interest into the life of this towering Jewish personality — Rabbi Moshe ben Maimon. It is in response to this interest that we publish this biography.

The biography is excerpted from "Our People," Vol. 5, published by Merkos L'inyonei Chinuch, in 1981. The text has been slightly emended and supplemented. Credit for the bulk of the text is due Rabbi Nissen Mangel, with editorial assistance by Rabbis Yosef Friedman and Meir Ossey.

It is hoped that this brief biographical sketch will whet the appetite of the reader and encourage him/her to learn more about the Rambam. It is also hoped that it will promote participation in the daily Rambam study program, thereby enhancing the knowledge and daily observance of the Mitzvot.

MERKOS L'INYONEI CHINUCH

Brooklyn, New York
Nissan 11, 5745
April 2, 1985

Rabbi Moshe ben Maimon was one of the towering figures in the history of the Jewish people. Of him it was said, "From Moshe (Moses) to Moshe (ben Maimon) there arose none like Moshe." Among the Jewish people, he is known as the Rambam, an acronym for Rabbi Moshe ben (son of) Maimon (RaMBaM); while universally — for his fame and influence transcended that of his own people — he is called Maimonides, the Greek form of "the son of Maimon."

Unauthenticated, traditional portrait of Rambam, and authentic
facsimile of Rambam's signature

EARLY YEARS

Rambam was born on the fourteenth day of Nissan — the day before Passover — in the year 1135,[1] in Cordova, Spain. He was a descendent of a distinguished and scholarly family tracing its ancestry to Rabbi Yehudah HaNassi, the compiler of the *Mishnah,* and even further back to the royal house of King David. At the conclusion of his *Commentary on the Mishnah (Uktzin* 3:12), Rambam enumerates his ancestry eight generations back, indicating that all were distinguished *Dayanim*, Rabbis and scholars. His father served as *Dayan* of the Jewish community of Cordova and was famous not only for his vast Torah knowledge, but also for his general scholarship, especially in mathematics and astronomy. Rabbi Maimon himself taught his prodigious son Scripture, Talmud, and every aspect of the Jewish religion and tradition, and provided him also with a multifaceted education and a thorough training in worldly sciences. It was at the suggestion of his father that the young Moshe immersed himself in the study of philosophy and medicine — fields in which he was to later attain world renown.

The young Moshe was barely Bar Mitzvah when the fanatical Almohades conquered Cordova in 1148. These ruthless, savage Moslems tolerated no other religion than their own and offered the Jewish population the choice of conversion to Islam, death, or expulsion from their native land. Thus the Jews were given the excruciating alternative of either surrendering their eternal faith or their very life, or abandoning their homeland where they had lived for many centuries, leaving behind all their possessions, to seek a haven of refuge in a hostile world where they were nowhere welcome. The vast majority of the Jews, among them the *Dayan* and his family, chose exile and left Cordova. Of those who could not leave, many met a martyr's death, sanctifying the Name of G-d, and some became insincere converts to Islam, merely outwardly, all the while, secretly, in their hearts and in the privacy of their homes, observing and practicing all the precepts of the Torah, never abandoning their inherited religion.

Rabbi Maimon and his family wandered about from city to city in Southern Spain, without being able to stay in any one place for a long period, for the conquering Almohadian hordes swept all across Southern Spain. After ten years of a nomadic life, they joined a group of fugitives who headed toward North Africa and eventually settled, in 1159, in Fez, then the capital of Morocco. But they were still not destined to enjoy peace and security. After a five year stay in Fez they had to leave because of religious intolerance and persecution. They again became wandering Jews, without a home. By way of Jerusalem and Hebron, the Maimon family made their way to Egypt. The Holy Land, desolate and unpopulated, ravaged by the Crusaders, did not afford them a permanent place of residence. They spent three days in Jerusalem in prayer at the Western Wall, and one day in Hebron praying at the graves of the Patriarchs at the Cave of Machpelah. From there they proceeded to Egypt. In Fostad, near Cairo, the seat of the Caliphate, the family of R. Maimon at last found a haven. Unlike other Moslem countries, the Jews in Egypt, under the tolerant and enlightened rule of the Fatimide caliphs, were granted complete religious and civil freedom. They were allowed to develop their religious, cultural and communal life, as well as to engage in commerce without any restrictions or interference. It was here that Rabbi Moshe was to create the masterworks for which the Jewish people are forever indebted to him.

In Egypt

They had barely settled in their new domicile, and

Maimonides Square with Monument to Rambam, Cordova, Spain

were just beginning to enjoy the long sought life of freedom and peace, when misfortune struck the Maimon family.

A few months after their arrival in Fostad, Rabbi Maimon, the former *Dayan* of Cordova, passed away. Rabbi Moshe deeply mourned the loss of his great father, who was to him not only a father but also his foremost teacher and most important influence.[2] His younger brother, David, took upon himself the responsibility of providing financial support for the entire family, in order to enable his gifted brother, Moshe, to devote himself to his studies without financial worry. David became a jewel merchant, importing gems and precious stones from India. He succeeded in this business and the family lived very comfortably. Unfortunately, the family was struck again by tragedy with the untimely death of their provider. On a business trip to India, the ship on which David was sailing was caught in a storm, shipwrecked in the Indian Ocean, and David drowned, carrying with him the entire family fortune.

It devolved upon Rabbi Moshe to become the breadwinner of the family. However, as a result of his incessant study and his grief over his brother's death, he became seriously ill. Bedridden for several months, he was unable to provide support for his family. When he finally recovered, he began to practice medicine. Rambam did not deem it proper to obtain monetary benefits or receive financial remuneration from his vast Torah knowledge. Torah should be studied and taught, he maintained, only for the sake of Heaven and not for earning a livelihood.[3] Hence he devoted himself to the vocation of medicine. He was so successful in this profession, and in the course of time gained such a reputation, that Grand Vizier Alfadhil, and eventually Sultan Saladin as well, appointed him to be their personal physician.

It is incumbent upon us to love and fear the glorious and awesome G-d, as it is written, "You shall love the L-rd your G-d" (Deut. 6:5), and "You shall fear the L-rd your G-d" (Deut. 6:13). How does one attain love and fear of G-d? When a person reflects upon His great, wondrous deeds and creatures, and from them perceives His infinite, unbounded wisdom, he will immediately be aroused to love, extol and glorify Him, and he will yearn with an exceeding yearning to know the Almighty G-d... By [further] meditating on these matters he will recoil, awe-stricken, resolving that he is a small, insignificant creature, endowed with limited, meager intelligence, who stands in the presence of the One who is perfect in knowledge...

Mishneh Torah, Yesodei HaTorah, 2:1-2

TALMUDIST

At the same time, Rabbi Moshe ben Maimon acquired world renown as a Talmudist of unusual knowledge and acumen. Scholars and Rabbis from all over the world sent him their halachic questions and queries. At the comparatively young age of forty-two, the Jewish community of Cairo appointed him as their Chief Rabbi, one of the most prestigious offices of the Jewish world at that time. Even before his formal appointment, his exceptional Torah scholarship and eminent personality made him the spiritual leader of Egyptian Jewry. When Rabbi Maimon's family settled in Egypt, the Karaites were in the majority and were more influential than those adhering to traditional Judaism. There was the danger that the large Jewish population of Egypt would be lost to Karaism. It was only a man of such great stature and authority as the Rambam who could stem the tide and eventually reverse it to traditional Judaism. In addition to his professional career as a physician and his voluntary activities as Chief Rabbi of the Jewish community, this great man still found time to study and to write masterful works on all branches of the Talmud, philosophy and medicine.

Commentary on the Mishnah

Rambam made three major contributions in the field of Jewish law and Talmudic study through his literary works: *Commentary on the Mishnah, Sefer HaMitzvot,* and *Mishneh Torah.* The earliest of these monumental works was his *Commentary on the Mishnah,* popularly known as *Sefer HaMaor* (The Luminary). He began this work at the age of twenty-three, while on his way fleeing the Mohammedan persecutions,

and completed it seven years later in Fostad. "I was working on this *Commentary* under the most arduous conditions... as we were driven from place to place... while
traveling by land or crossing the stormy sea," he writes at
the conclusion of this work. His clear, methodical and
analytical mind and his remarkable ability to arrange the
material systematically is already evident in this early
work. The *Commentary* offers brief explanations for each
Mishnah, in the six "Orders" which comprise the *Mishnah,*
elucidating the meaning of every dictum which is not per-
fectly clear from the text. These explanations are generally
gleaned from the vast material and the lengthy discussions
of the Talmud, and where no interpretation is found in the
Talmud, Rambam gives those of his predecessors, the *Gaonim,* or his own. Wherever necessary, he includes in his
commentary scientific information showing thereby that
the Sages of the Talmud were well-versed in all spheres of
secular knowledge. Besides its expository value, the *Commentary* has an added asset for the practical application of
the law. It delineates the final halachic decision from
among the various opinions mentioned in the *Mishnah.*

Rambam composed an elaborate Introduction to the
Commentary in which he discusses various fundamental concepts of the Jewish religion, such as prophecy, revelation
and tradition, the development and the principles of the
Oral Law,[4] and the like. He also wrote individual introdu-
tions to all difficult sections of the *Mishnah* and to all
complicated subjects treated in the *Mishnah,* clearly elucidating the pertinent principles underlying the laws and
furnishing a concise summary of all the relevant halachic
concepts. All this precedes the detailed commentary which
explains the meaning of the Mishnaic text.

Thirteen Principles of Faith

One of the most famous and significant of Rambam's
Introductions is his preface to the tenth chapter of the
tractate *Sanhedrin.* There he formulates the "Thirteen Prin-

Facsimile of the manuscript of Rambam's *Commentary on the Mishnah* in Arabic with Hebrew characters, in his own handwriting

ciples of the Jewish Faith." These fundamental principles of Judaism have been incorporated into the liturgy of many Jewish communities, reciting them at the beginning of the daily morning prayer, in poetical form (*Yigdal*), and at the end, in prose form — *Ani Maamin*.

The first five of these cardinal principles deal with the existence of G-d the Creator, His Oneness, His incorporeality, His eternity, and the principle that all prayer and worship are due G-d alone. The next four principles pertain to prophecy in general, and the unique, pre-eminent level of Moshe Rabbeinu's prophecy, the Divine origin of the Torah in its immutability. Principle ten and eleven affirm G-d's omniscience and the certainty of reward and punishment for observance or transgression of the mitzvot. The final two principles deal with the Messianic redemption and the resurrection of the dead.

Equally famous is Rambam's Introduction to *Pirkei Avot,* the Talmudic tractate which deals with ethical behavior. Although it is only an introduction to *Pirkei Avot* and but a small part of his *Commentary on the Mishnah,* it is, nevertheless, a highly significant ethical treatise in its own right. Popularly known as *Shemoneh Perakim* (Eight Chapters), this treatise has been translated into many languages. In it Rabbi Moshe ben Maimon offers a systematic presentation of the foundations of Jewish ethics, and discusses such basic Jewish concepts as the nature of the soul, its maladies and cures, immortality, freedom of will, freedom of choice and Divine foreknowledge, and similar topics touched upon in *Pirkei Avot.*

His Talmudic genius is especially evident in his Introduction and Commentary to *Seder Taharot* (Order of Purity), which comprises twelve tractates of the most complicated laws of purity and impurity. Rambam's Introduction and Commentary succeeded in making these intricate tractates of Mishnah accessible and readily comprehensible.

The *Commentary* was written in the Arabic vernacular,

ANI MAAMIN — I BELIEVE

Based on the Thirteen Principles of Faith formulated by the Rambam in his Commentary on the Mishnah Sanhedrin 10:1.

1. I believe with complete faith that the Creator, blessed be His name, is the Creator and Guide of all the created beings, and that He alone has made, does make, and will make all things.
2. I believe with complete faith that the Creator, blessed be His name, is One and Alone; that there is no oneness in any way like Him; and that He alone is our G-d — was, is and will be.
3. I believe with complete faith that the Creator, blessed be His name, is incorporeal; that He is free from all anthropomorphic properties; and that He has no likeness at all.
4. I believe with complete faith that the Creator, blessed be His name, is the first and the last.
5. I believe with complete faith that the Creator, blessed be His name, is the only one to whom it is proper to pray, and that it is inappropriate to pray to anyone else.
6. I believe with complete faith that all the words of the Prophets are true.

7. I believe with complete faith that the prophecy of Moses our teacher, peace unto him, was true; and that he was the father of the prophets, both of those who preceded and of those who followed him.

8. I believe with complete faith that the whole Torah which we now possess was given to Moses, our teacher, peace unto him.

9. I believe with complete faith that this Torah will not be changed, and that there will be no other Torah given by the Creator, blessed be His name.

10. I believe with complete faith that the Creator, blessed be His name, knows all the deeds and thoughts of human beings, as it is said, "It is He who fashions the hearts of them all, He who perceives all their actions." (Psalms 33:15).

11. I believe with complete faith that the Creator, blessed be His name, rewards those who observe His commandments, and punishes those who transgress His commandments.

12. I believe with complete faith in the coming of *Mashiach,* and although he may tarry, nevertheless, I wait every day for him to come.

13. I believe with complete faith that there will be resurrection of the dead at the time when it will be the will of the Creator, blessed be His name and exalted be His remembrance forever and ever.

the language the masses understood, and called *Kiteb El Siraj* (The Luminary). Later, successive parts were rendered into Hebrew by various scholars. The popularity of this work can be seen from the fact that it is appended to every complete edition of the Talmud.

Even before he began his *Commentary on the Mishnah*, i.e., before the age of twenty-three, Rambam was an accomplished author. His first known works were *Ma'amar Halbbur*, a treatise on the Jewish calendar in which he demonstrates a profound knowledge of astronomy and mathematics, and *Beur Millot HaHigayon*, a philosophic dissertation on logic, both of which survive in Hebrew translation. He composed also a commentary on almost three entire *sedarim* (Orders) of the Babylonian Talmud, viz., *Moed, Nashim,* and *Nezikin,* as well as on the tractate of *Chulin,* and wrote a halachic digest of the Jerusalem Talmud similar to that which Rabbi Yitzchak Alfasi wrote on the Babylonian Talmud. Neither of the Talmudic commentaries — with the exception of a few tractates — are extant. The halachic digest which was heretofore never published, and thought to be lost, was recently discovered and published for the first time in 1947 in New York. That he could create all this, still in his teens, under the most trying circumstances, while fleeing from country to country, without having at his disposal all the necessary books is all the more incredible!

Truth does not become more true by virtue of the fact that the entire world agrees with it, nor less so even if the whole world disagrees with it.

Moreh Nevuchim 2:15

CODIFICATION OF JEWISH LAW

Had the Rambam written no other work but the *Commentary on the Mishnah*, it would have been sufficient to immortalize him among the Jewish people. But he had no sooner completed this work than he embarked on his next and even more ambitious project, the codification of Jewish law.

Some years earlier Rabbi Yitzchak Alfasi (known as the "Rif") took the first major step in codifying the laws of the Talmud. It was beyond the ability of the average person, indeed of anyone except the greatest scholar, to determine directly from the Talmud with its numerous opinions and diverse views, the final halachic ruling on any given matter. R. Yitzchak Alfasi gleaned the legal passages and authoritative opinions of the Talmud, deleting the intricate discussion of the Amoraim and all non-halachic material, and organized them in more or less the same order and form, quoting them in the very words as they were presented in the Talmud, and, where necessary, indicating the *halachah*. This was, indeed, a monumental achievement in determining the final, definitive *halachah*. His method of codification, however, followed the arrangement of the Talmud, not a topical system, where all laws of the same subject are grouped under the same head. As the years passed, the pressing need for a more systematically arranged, clear-cut, practical code was increasingly felt. It was the crowning accomplishment of Rabbi Moshe ben Maimon to present the first comprehensive, all-encompassing, topically arranged code of Jewish law, distinguished by matchless clarity and lucidity. In the words of the Rambam himself, in his Introduction to *Mishneh Torah:*

> ...At this time, the sufferings of our people have increased. The pressing need of the moment supersedes every other consideration. The wisdom of the wise has vanished, and the wisdom of our learned men is concealed. Hence, the commentaries, compilations of laws and Responsa of the Gaonim, which they thought were easy to understand, have in our times become difficult to understand, and there are only a few individuals who are able to comprehend them properly.... For this reason, I, Moshe ben Maimon, the Sephardi, have girded my loins and relying on the help of the Almighty, blessed be He, have thoroughly studied all their works and decided to compile the results derived from them as to what is prohibited and what is unclean, and all the other laws of the Torah, all in clear language and concise style, so that the entire oral Torah will be systematically arranged for all. [I shall not quote] the questions and answers or the differences of opinion discussed... but only the laws themselves in a clear and succinct manner, in accordance with the conclusions derived from all these treatises and compilations existing since the time of Rabbi Yehudah HaNassi until the present day — so that all the laws shall be accessible to young and old, whether they are Biblical precepts or enactments by the sages or Prophets. In short, [my purpose in composing this code is] that no man shall have any need to resort to any other book on any matter of Jewish law, but that this compendium contain the entire Oral Law, including the ordinances, customs and decrees instituted from the time of Moshe Rabbeinu to the redaction of the Talmud, and as expounded for us by the Gaonim in all their works composed by them since the completion of the Talmud. Therefore, I called this work *Mishneh Torah* (Second Law to the Torah), for a man should first read the Written Torah and then read this code and he will know from it the entire Oral Law without the need of reading any other book between them.

Facsimile of a page from the manuscript of Rambam's *Mishneh Torah*,
end of *Hilchot Sechirot*, in his own handwriting

Sefer HaMitzvot

Before commencing the monumental task of codifying the whole range of halachic material contained in the Biblical, Talmudic and Gaonic literature, the Rambam composed another halachic work, called *Sefer HaMitzvot* (The Book of the Commandments). It is a sort of introduction to the *Mishneh Torah*, but is also a valuable work in its own right and is the second of his three major works on *halachah*, the other two being his Mishnaic *Commentary* and the *Mishneh Torah*.

The main objective of *Sefer HaMitzvot* is to enumerate the six hundred thirteen precepts contained in the Torah. The Sages of the Talmud speak of 613 *Mitzvot*, i.e., the six hundred thirteen Biblical commandments. These are subdivided into two hundred forty-eight positive precepts *(mitzvot aseh)* and three hundred sixty-five negative or prohibitory precepts *(lo ta'aseh or lav)*. A simple, superficial counting of the Biblical laws, however, yields a substantially larger number than six hundred thirteen. Nowhere in the Talmud is there a detailed enumeration given of these injuctions and prohibitions nor an explicit formulation of the principles and rules on the basis of which Biblical laws should be counted.

The Rambam divided his *Sefer* into two sections. The first is a profound exposition of the theoretical basis that guided him in determining those particular *mitzvot* which were to be included or excluded from the list of Biblical precepts. It presents and explains fourteen rules and principles according to which the Biblical injunctions and prohibitions should be counted. He establishes each of these principles and proves them with an abundance of evidence from the entire Talmudic literature. In the second section, the Rambam enumerates and defines the six hundred thirteen commandments, which are, in turn, divided into two hundred forty-eight affirmative precepts and three hundred sixty-five prohibitory injunctions.

This work, as all works of the Rambam, has enjoyed great popularity throughout the ages and many commentaires were written on it. The current standard edition of *Sefer HaMitzvot* is printed with seven commentaries.

Mishneh Torah

At the age of thirty-two,[5] Rabbi Moshe ben Maimon began working on the *Mishneh Torah,* and it took him ten years[6] of intensive uninterrupted labor to complete this monumental work. It was an extraordinry feat to codify the vast material in the Talmud even in ten years. It is told that when Rambam completed the work, his father, R. Maimon and another man appeared to him in a dream. "This is Moshe Rabbeinu," his father informed him. Rambam was awe-stricken. "I have come to see the work which you have written," said Moshe Rabbeinu. He examined the Code and said, *"Yeyasher kochacha;* it is a work well done!"

Whereas the *Commentary on the Mishnah* and the *Sefer HaMitzvot,* as well as all his other major and minor treatises, were written in Arabic, Rambam wrote the *Mishneh Torah,* his greatest work, in Hebrew, for it was meant not only for the Arabic-speaking Jewry. It was designed to last beyond such transitory periods as the stay of the Jewish people within the orbit of Arabic culture; it was composed for all times — even for the Messianic Era — and for all places. And for this, only the Holy Tongue would be the proper vehicle. When he was requested to translate this work into Arabic, he expressed regret that he did not write his other works in Hebrew; he would prefer to have his Arabic writings rendered into Hebrew rather than the reverse.

The *Mishneh Torah* is composed in a lucid, well-styled Hebrew. Scholars of later generations have referred to the Rambam's *lashon hazahav* — "golden language," a beautiful syntax and above all a precise, unambiguous, clear style and language in which there is nothing superfluous or redundant. "Had I been able to put the entire Oral Torah into one chapter, I would not have used two," Rambam once said. His choice of words is so precise that many a law which is not mentioned explicitly in his Code was deduced merely from the manner of his expressions.

Unlike the earlier codifiers who used the Talmud as the model for their halachic compendia as far as language, structure and organization of the laws are concerned, Rabbi Moshe ben Maimon used the *Mishnah* as the model for his. The *Mishnah* is divided into *Sedarim* (Orders); each order into tractates; each tractate into chapters; each chapter into halachic sections called *Mishnayot*. Similarly, the Rambam divided *Mishneh Torah* into fourteen books; each book into sections of related laws; each section into chapters; and each chapter into individual *halachot*. This is of course a more logical organization and methodical presentation and makes it much easier to locate the specific topic of law which one seeks. Although Rabbi Moshe gave this work the formal title *Mishneh Torah,* it also came to be known as *Yad HaChazakah* (The Mighty Hand)[7] because of the divisions of the work into fourteen books — "*Yad*" having the numerical value of fourteen (*yud* equals to 10 and *daled* to 4).

The uniqueness of *Mishneh Torah* or *Yad HaChazakah* lies not only in its systematic arrangement, lucid presentation and stylistic beauty, but also in the scope of its content. The *Mishneh Torah* is the only complete code which contains all the Biblical, Talmudic and Gaonic legislation, including the laws which cannot be observed since the destruction of the *Bet Hamikdash*. The Code of the Rif, as well as those of other codifiers who preceded or followed the Rambam, including the *Shulchan Aruch,* left out all such *halachot* which cannot be practiced in post-exilic times. Rabbi Moshe ben Maimon, however, included in his Code the entire range of Jewish law, the Written and Oral law, even that which cannot be observed until the coming of *Mashiach*. Thus the *Yad HaChazakah* is valid for Jewish life in exile, as it will be in the time of *Mashiach* when the Jewish People will once again be able to bring offerings in the Holy Temple and the

Sanhedrin will be restored. Herein lies one of the most significant values of *Mishneh Torah*.

Opposition to Mishneh Torah

From the moment of its appearance, *Mishneh Torah* won immediate acclaim; it was hailed as the foremost achievement of Torah scholarship in post-Talmudic times. At the same time, however, this monumental work aroused strong opposition on the part of some individuals. Some critics opposed the Code on the ground that it would jeopardize the study of the Talmud. They feared that this codification of the entire Written and Oral Law would make the study of the Talmud less necessary, if not altogether superfluous. To substantiate their fear, they cited Rambam's own words in his Introdution to *Mishneh Torah:* "Therefore I called the work *Mishneh Torah,* for a man should first read the Written Torah and then read this code and he will know from it the entire Oral law, without the need of reading any other book." He makes the same statement in this regard in his Introduction to the *Sefer HaMitzvot.* One may mistakenly infer from this, his critics feared, that merely studying the Code together with Scripture would provide a Jew with adequate knowledge of Torah law.

Others critized the Rambam for his failure to indicate the sources of his halachic decisions. The Code simply states the law without quoting references to its sources. Another charge levelled against Rabbi Moshe ben Maimon was that he does not give the reasons for the laws. Not knowing the reason for the *halachah* or from where it is derived, his critics claimed, one can easily misunderstand or misapply the law, especially if one applies it to a superficially similar situation. Indeed, some Rabbis forbade one to derive a legal ruling from the Code without being familiar with the sources.

All this opposition, however, did not diminish the respect for *Mishneh Torah,* nor the universal admiration for

אז לא אבוש בהביטי אל כל מצותיך

כל המצות

שניתנו לו למשה בסיני
בפירושן ניתנו שנאמר
ואתנה לך את לוחות
האבן והתורה והמצוה
תורה זו תורה שבכתב
והמצוה זו פירוש וצונו
לעשות התורה על פי
המצו. ומצוה זו היא הנקרא תורה שבעל פה · כל התור
כתבה משה רבינו קורם שימות בכתב ידו · ונתן ספר
לכל שבט ושבט וספר אחד נתנהו בארון לעד שנאמר
לקוח את ספר התורה הוה ושמתם אותו וגו · והמצוה
שהיא פירוש התורה לא כתבה · אלא צוה בה לזקנים
וליהושע ולשאר כל ישראל שנאמר את כל הדבר אשר
אנכי מצוה אתכם תשמרו לעשות וגום · ומפני זה
נקראת תורה שבעל פה : אף על פי שלא
נכתבה תורה שבעל פה למדה משה רבינו כולה בבית
דינו לשבעים זקנים · ואלעזר ופנחס ויהושע שלשתן
קבלו ממשה · וליהושע שהוא תלמירו שלמשה רבינו
מסר תורה שבעל פה וצוהו עליה · וכן יהושע כל ימי
חייו למד על פה וזקנים רבים קבלו מיהושע וקבל על
מן הזקנים ופנחס ושמואל קיבל מעלי ובית דינו ודוד
קיבל משמוא ובֿ · ואחיה השילוני מיוצאי מצרים היה
ולוי היה ושמע ממשה והוא בימי משה קטן והוא קיבל
מרור ובית דינו ואליהו קיבל מאחיה השילוני ובי דינו
ואלישע קיבל מאליהו ובית דינו · ויהוירע הכהן קיבל
מאלישע ובית דינו וזכריה קיבל מיהוירע ובית דינו
והושע קיבל מזכריה ובית דינו · ועמוס קיבל מהושע
ובית דינו וישעיה קיבל מעמוס ובית דינו ומיכה קיבל
מישעיה ובית דינו ויואל קיבל ממיכה ובית דינו ונחום
קיבל מיוא ובית דינו · וחבקוק קיבל מנחום ובית דינו
וצפניה קיבל מחבקוק ובית דינו וירמיה קיבל מצפניה
ובית דינו · וברוך בן נריה קבלו מברוך בן נריה ובית
דינו שלעזרא הם הנקראי אנשי כנסת הגדולה והם חגי

שא גאולת עולם תהיה ללויים   ישרא שרש את אבי
אמו לוי   הרי זה גוו מלוי אעפ שאינו לוי הואיל והוארי
או השרות של לויים גוו לעולם   שרין זה תלוי בסקומות
או ולא בבעלים ולוי שרש את אבי אמו ישרא גוו כישרא
ולא מלוים שלא נאמר גאולת עולם תהיה ללויים בערי
הלויים
כנען וכן הן מוזהרין שלא ינחלו בארץ
את הערים שנאמר לא יהיה לכהני הלוי כל שבט לוי חלק
ונחלה עם ישרא חלק ונחלה בארץ וכן הוא אומר
בארץ לא תנחל וחלק לא יהיה לך בתוכם בבוה וכן לוי
או כהן שנטל חלק בבוה לוקה ואם נטל נחלה בארץ
מעבירי אותה ממנו יראה לי שאין הרברי אוסרין
לא בארץ שנכרתה עליה ברית לאברהם ליצחק
וליעק וירשוה בניה ונתחלקה להם אבל שאר
כל הארצות שכיבש שלך ממלך ישראל
הרי הכהני והלויי כאיתן הארצן ובניתן
בכל ישרא ולמה לא זכה לוי בנחלת
ארץ ישראל ובבותה עם אחיו מפני
שהובדל לעבור את ה ולשרתו
ולהורו דרכיו הישרן ומשפטיו
הצריקים לרבים שנא יורו
משפטך ליעקב ותורתך
לישרא לפי הובדלו
סדרכי העול לא
עורכין
מלחמה כשאר
ישרא ולא נוחלין
ולא זוכין לעצמן
בכח גופן אא הם חיל
ה שנאמ ברך ה חילו והוא
ברוך הוא זוכה להם שנ אני
חלקך ונחלתך ולא שבט לוי
בלבד אא כל איש ואיש מכל באי
העולם אשר נרבה רוח אותו והבינו
מרעו להבדל לעמור לפני ה לשרתו
ולעברו לדעה את ה והלך ישר כמו שעשהו
האלהים ופרק מעל צואריו עול החשבונות הרבי
אשר בקש בני הארם   הרי זה נתקרש קורש
קרשים ויהיה ה חלקו   ונחלתו לעולם ולעולמי
עולמים ויזכה לו בעולם רבר המספיק לו כמו שכה
לכהנים וללויים הרי רוד עליו השלום אומ ה מנת חלקי
וכוסי אתה תומיך גורלי

From the first complete printed edition of *Mishneh Torah*, Rome, ca. 1480

it. Its deficiencies — the omission of the references to the sources, as well as the reasons for the *halachot* — were remedied by a number of commentators on the Code, chief among them R. Joseph Karo in his *Keseph Mishneh*.[8] The fear that the Code would wean scholars away from the study of the Talmud, was, in retrospect, completely unwarranted. It not only did not weaken or discourage the study of the Talmud; on the contrary, it enhanced it. For to understand the Code properly, to perceive the profundity hidden in each phrase, one must immerse oneself in the study of the Talmud.

Each one of the six hundred thirteen precepts serves either to inculcate proper attitudes or to remove some erroneous conceptions, to establish just legislation or to eliminate iniquity, to imbue one with exemplary virtues or to deter one from evil dispositions.

Moreh Nevuchim 3:31

The foundation of all foundations [and basic principles of the Torah] and the pillar of all wisdoms is to know that there is a First Being Who brings every existing thing into being. All existing things — in heaven, on earth and what is between them — come into being only from His true existence.

If it should enter one's mind that He does not exist — no other thing could have any existence.

Mishneh Torah, Yesodei HaTorah, 1:1-2

RESPONSA

Besides the aforementioned three major works of Rabbi Moshe ben Maimon, he also composed numerous *Teshuvot* (Responsa) to the queries addressed to him for his opinion and authoritative decision, from all centers of Jewish settlement. With the appearance of his first major work the *Commentary on the Mishnah*, Rambam was regarded as one of the leading authorities on Jewish law and religion. With the appearance of *Mishneh Torah*, he was further recognized as the most authoritative Jewish scholar of his time. Literally thousands of inquiries were directed to him concerning all areas of Jewish life. His *Teshuvot* include answers to specific questions of Jewish law, religious and civil; explanations of difficult Talmudic and Aggadaic passages; discussions of theological and religio-philosophical matters, as well as all the burning issues of the times.

Many of the Responsa were written in Arabic and later translated into Hebrew. On the whole, they are brief and concise, in contrast to the responsa of later generations which are characterized by the dialectic, *pilpul* approach. Some *teshuvot* are so terse that they are limited to a few words, or even just to "permissible" or "forbidden." Other queries, however, were of such vital importance, that Rambam responded to them at great length and in great detail, to such an extent that they have become important texts themselves in Jewish religious literature.

Iggeret Hashmad

One of these historical epistles is the *Iggeret HaShmad* (Epistle Concerning Apostasy). It is also known by the title *Maamar Kiddush Hashem* (Discourse on Martyrdom — the

Sanctificaton of the Name of G-d). The fanatical Almohades, who ruled not only in Spain but also in North Africa, tolerated no other religion but Islam. Adoption of Mohammedanism, expulsion, or a martyr's death were the only choices granted to the "infidel." Many Jews gave up personal comfort, property and possessions and fled the region. Some feigned belief in the dominant religion, while inwardly remaining loyal Jews, and secretly, in the privacy of their homes, observed all the laws and precepts of the Torah. In the epistle *Iggeret HaShmad*, Rabbi Moshe ben Maimon discusses the halachic status of these unfortunate Islamic "marranos" or secret Jews — whether or not they are considered apostates and idolators, albeit involuntary. This specific problem affords the Rambam the opportunity to treat the matter of apostacy at length. He discusses what makes one an apostate. Under what conditions must one give up his life for his religion? Does the *halachah* differentiate between one who merely pays lip service to the enforced religion while secretly observing all the *mitzvot* and one who is coerced to transgress Torah law in action? He also discusses what constitutes sanctification *(Kiddush HaShem)* or desecration of G-d's Name *(Chilul HaShem)*. The epistle was originally written in Arabic and later translated into Hebrew.

Iggeret Teiman

An even more famous letter by Rambam, *Iggeret Teiman* (Epistle Concerning Yemen), was composed as the result of similar persecutions in another Jewish community. This epistle was written in reponse to a query by a Yemenite sage, Rabbi Jacob al-Fayumi during a period of violent persecution and religious intolerance in his country. About the year 1168, the Jews of Yemen were confronted with a three-pronged agonizing problem. A fanatical Moslem cleric became the ruler of this distant, primitive South Arabian land and decreed that his Jewish subjects convert to Islam under the threat of harsh punishment and suffer-

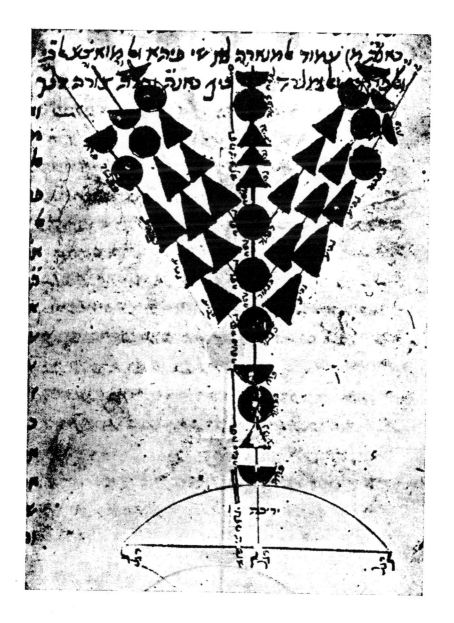

Facsimile of Rambam's own sketch of the Menorah (candelabra) in
the *Bet Hamikdash*

ing. Their agony was compounded by a Jewish apostate who embraced Mohammedanism. To demonstrate his zeal for his newly adopted faith, he began preaching to the Jewish communities that Mohammed was a divinely sent prophet alluded to in the Bible and that Islam was a new, divinely revealed religion superseding Judaism. Hence, the apostate argued, the Jews should yield to the ruler's demand and embrace Mohammedanism. Furthermore, at just about this time, an impostor appeared proclaiming himself to be the Messiah, adding to the confusion of the poor wretched masses. Rabbi Jacob al-Fayumi turned to Rambam for advice and counsel.

Rabbi Moshe ben Maimon addressed a letter to this sage, and through him to the entire Jewish population of Yemen. He states that the root of all anti-Semitism throughout the ages is envy in the Jews being the Chosen People and the recipients of the G-d given Torah. Unable to do battle with the Almighty Himself, the haters turn their jealous rage toward His people. Throughout the ages this has taken three forms: brute force to exterminate the physical existence of the Chosen People; sophisticated persuasions to refute or falsify the teachings of Judaism, epitomized by Hellenism; and finally by the combination of the two, the false claims of new religions — Christianity and Islam — that Judaism is no longer valid and Jews must be forced to accept the new revelation. He consoled them by telling them that the Jews are a unique and indestructible nation; that all the past and present sufferings and persecutions were foretold by the Prophets, and just as in the past the nations had failed to annihilate the Jewish people or destroy the Jewish religion, so will the present persecution fail, and peace and tranquility will return to the community. He contemptuously dismissed and disproved the assertion that Judaism has been supplanted by Islam and showed that the claim that Mohammed is alluded to in the Bible is based upon nonsensical interpretations recognized as such even by the Moslems themselves.

Rambam advised that the self-proclaimed Messiah is nothing but an impostor and no doubt a madman. He urged them to remain firm in the belief that G-d will send the true *Mashiach* to redeem the Jewish people from suffering in exile at the proper time.

The epistle accomplished its purpose — the Yemenite Jews remained faithful to their religion in the face of their bitter suffering. Rabbi Moshe ben Maimon used his influence at the court of Saladin in Egypt to intervene in their behalf, and the persecution came to an end. The Jewish community of Yemen gratefully appreciated both the spiritual advice as well as the actual help of Rambam in the hour of their distress and honored him by including his name in the *Kaddish* prayer, saying: "May He establish His kingship... in your lifetime and in the lifetime of the entire House of Israel *and in the lifetime of Rabbeinu Moshe ben Maimon*," an honor theretofore reserved for the *Resh Galutah* (Jewish Exilarch) in Babylonia.

There are things which are within the scope and capacity of the human mind to grasp; there are things which the mind can in no way and by no means fathom — the gates of perception are closed against it.

Moreh Nevuchim 1:31

PHILOSOPHER
AND MYSTIC

Rabbi Moshe ben Maimon was not only the leading Talmudic and Halachic personality of his time, but also the chief exponent of Jewish religious philosophy. After concluding his *magnum opus*, the *Mishneh Torah*, Rambam set out to present the religious philosophical views of Judaism. These he elaborated on in his masterly philosophic treatise, *Moreh Nevuchim* (Guide for the Perplexed), wherein he deals comprehensively with Jewish doctrine and practice from a philosophical point of view.

Moreh Nevuchim

In this work, Rambam provides answers to the perennial questions for which the human mind ever searches: the nature and existence of G-d, the purpose of Creation, G-d and His relation to the universe, the meaning of life and human destiny, the origin and underlying reality of evil, free will, Divine Providence and Omniscience, Divine Justice, Revelation, the purpose of the precepts of the Torah, the true way of worshipping G-d, and many others.

In the countries under Islamic cultural influence, such as Egypt where Rambam lived, where Greek philosophy captured the imagination of the intelligentsia, it became popular also in certain Jewish circles. With the growing interest in the works of the ancient Greek philosopher Aristotle, especially in its Arabic garb and formulation, there arose an apparent conflict between the views of secular philosophy and certain statements and ideas expressed in the Torah and Talmudic literature. For instance, how can G-d's absolute incorporeality and spirituality be reconciled with the anthropomorphic, human descriptions of Him in the Bible. The philosophically oriented Jews, while firmly committed to the principles and practice of Torah Judaism, were troubled and perplexed by the seeming contradiction between reason and faith. Rambam, in his deep-felt concern for the spiritual well-being of his people, recognized the inherent danger to which such a situation might lead. This danger was especially acute among the less educated in Jewish religious thought among whom Aristotelian philosophy threatened to make serious inroads and who, as a result of the apparent inconsistencies between reason and faith, began to waver in their religious commitment. Rabbi Moshe ben Maimon, well-versed in the teachings of the ancient and contemporary philosophers, therefore, felt himself compelled to compose a systematic presentation and exposition of the fundamental religio-philosophical principles of Judaism, which would answer the questions which agitated the philosophically oriented intellectuals, remove the doubts of the "perplexed" and enable them to continue to adhere to Torah-true Judaism. "My intention," says the Rambam in the introduction to *Moreh Nevuchim,* "is... to expound Biblical passages which had been impugned, and to elucidate their hidden and true meaning which when well-understood, serve as a means to remove the doubts concerning anything taught in Scripture; and, indeed, many difficulties will disappear when that which I am about to explain is taken into consideration."

The *Moreh Nevuchim* was originally written in Arabic with Hebrew characters, and titled *Dalalat al-Chairin.* No sooner had the work been completed than the author was besieged with requests from various centers of Jewish scholarship for copies of his latest work, and for a Hebrew translation for the benefit of those unfamiliar with the language in which it was written. Within a decade after its

מורה נבוכים חלק ראשון פרק א

שיר מרובע ותשבע שחבר הרב ז"ל:

דעי הולך, לנתות דרך, ישר לסלול, את מסלולה:
הוי כל תועה, בשדה תורה, סורה ודרוך, יד מעגלה:
טמא וכסיל, לא יעבור בה, דרך קודש, יקרא לה:

פרק א — צלם ודמות

א כבר חשבו בני אדם, כי צלם בלשון העברי יורה על תמונת הדבר ותארו, והביא זה אל הגשמה גמורה, לאמרו: נעשה אדם בצלמנו כדמותנו. וחשבו שהשם על צורת אדם ר"ל תמונתו ותארו, והתחייבה להם ההגשמה הגמורה, והאמינו בה, וראו שהם אם יפרדו מזאת האמונה יכזיבו הכתוב. ב וגם ישימו השם נעדר, אם לא יהיה גוף בעל פנים ויד כמותם בתמונה ובתאר, אלא שהוא יותר גדול ויותר בהיר לפי סברתם, והחמר שלו גם כן אינו דם ובשר. זה תכלית מה שחשבוהו רוממות בחק השם. ג אמנם מה שצריך שיאמר בהרחקת הגשמות, והעמיד האחדות האמיתית, (אשר אין אמת לה אלא בהסרת הגשמות) הנה תדע המופת על כל זה מזה המאמר (פרק מ"ו חלק א'), אבל הערתנו הנה בזה הפרק, היא לבאר ענין צלם דמות. ואומר כי הצורה המפורסמת אצל ההמון, אשר

אפודי

פרק ראשון א כבר חשבו בני אדם רוצה לומר הדמיון ההמוני. והביא זה אל ההגשמה הגמורה ר"ל שלא יחייב היותו כח בגשם וזהו אומרו גמורה: ב וגם ישימו השם נעדר וכו'. ר"ל שאלו האנשים הסכלים האמינו בהגשמה מצד שני דברים. האחת מהם שנתפשו אחר פשוטי הכתוב ואם יפרדו מזאת האמונה יכזיבו הכתובים לפי דעתם. והשנית מצד שכלם העכור והמבולבל ישימו הש"י נעדר אם לא יהיה גוף אפילו לא יהיה להם פשטי התורה כי לפי דעתם מה שאינו גשם או כח בגשם אינו נמצא: ג אמנם מה שצריך וכו' ר"ל עכשיו בא המורה לסתור דעתם בהאמנת ההגשמה מצד השני דברים שהאמינו בה אלו הסכלים. ואמר אמנם שצריך להביא מופת עכשיו שהש"י אינו גשם עד דעת מה שחייב שכלם העכור מאלו הסכלים אין זה מקומו ויתבאר בראש חלק ב'. אבל תהיה הערתנו בזה הפרק לדחות מאלו הסכלים האמנת ההגשמה מצד הפסוקים שהאמינו שלא יפרדו מזאת האמונה

שם טוב

פרק ראשון צלם ודמות. אמר הרב צלם ודמות כבר חשבו בני אדם, הפירוש כבר ביארנו בפתיחת זה הספר כי הפשטת הגשמות מהאל יתברך אינו מכלל הסתרים אשר ראוי להעלים אבל בהרחקת הגשמות ראוי שישותפו ההמון והחכמים ויחנכו הנערים ג"כ כמו שביאר הרב בפרק ל"ה, ולמה שימלאו סתרים רבים יחוייב שיקבל אותם החכם אחר קבלת שהשם אינו גשם, ראה הרב בעבור שני אלו הטעמים לסלק הגשמות, והתחיל בצלם למה שאדון הנביאים התחיל בו במעשה בראשית גם כי הוא כולל כל חלקי ההגשמה כמו שביאר החכם רבי משה הנרבוני: ואמר כבר חשבו בני אדם כי צלם בלשון עברי יורה על תמונת הדבר ותוארו. והרצון בו כי צלם יורה על תמונה ותואר, כבר ידעת כי תמונה ותאר הם ממאמר האיכות והם ממקרי הכמות במה שהוא כמות ואם הדבר כן מה שאמר במעשה בראשית נעשה

אברבנאל

צלם ודמות וכו'. הנה התחיל הרב בביאור הזה שהוא ענין מענייני מעשה בראשית, לפי שהשם אדוננו כי התחיל התורה גם כן, וגם כן להיות כולל כל חלקי ההגשמה. ואולי עוד לסבה שלישית, והיא לבאר שהאדם נאמר שהוא בצלם אלהים מפני ההשגה השכלית אשר לו וע"כ ראוי שישים כל בהשתדלותו בעיוניות, יען מפני זה נאמר עליו שהוא בצלם אלהים. והנרבוני כתב שהתחיל בזה כי הוא התכלית וראשית המחשבה אחרית המעשה והיא כולל כל חלקי ההגשמה. והוא ירצה שהתחיל הרב בביאור צלם לפי שהוא התכלית באדם ר"ל ההשגה השכלית, שכיון במלת צלם. ושם הרב ראשית המחשבה כל התחלת מחשבתו ועיונו מה הספר במה שהוא אחרית המעשה באדם והיא ההשכלה שנקראת צלם. ולאשר לומר שכיון ג"כ הנרבוני לומר שהתחיל הרב בפתח בצלם ובהם בארו בדרך החכמה ובניהם אחד, וראשית המחשבה סוף המעשה, וזו סבה אחת. אחר זו זכר סבה אחרת שנייה, והיא אמרו: והוא כולל כל חלקי ההגשמה: כבר חשבו כו'. מה שלא אמר כשאר המתפיסים להעיר על האומרים שיש אל אחד אבל שהוא גוף ובעל תמונה ושהביאים ראיה מפסוק נעשה אדם בצלמנו כדמותנו בחשבם שצלם ודמות נאמרו על תמונת הדבר ותאריו ומקריו, ועליהם אמר כבר חשבו בני אדם. והמתפיסים שלשה ענינים ידקו נגד האומן שמותם בלשון הרב, ושני השמות האלה צלם ודמות, הם מחולקים בלשונותיהם, על כן בני אדם האלה בוכיתו הדבר מלשון עברי, ולפי שהיה כוונתו להעיר על מה שאמרתי, אמר הרב, והביא זה אל ההגשמה גמורה לאמרו נעשה אדם בצלמנו כדמותנו וחשבו שהשם על צורת אדם, עם היות שהביא ג"כ דעת אחרים שהגדילו גשמות האלוה ואמרו שאינו בעל ידים ופנים כמו שיזכור: והתחייבה כו'. אל החשוב שיכוין הרב בלשון הזה שמדעת בני אדם שזכר יתחייב ויתבאר גשמות האל ית', כי הם אמרוהו בפירוש ואין יאמר הרב שיתבאר ויתחייב לדעתם כאלו הם לא בארוהו, אבל יאמר הרב שמה שאמרו בני אדם מזה לא נצלו עליו באפשרות הסברא, והשוו אליה, אבל היה זה בעיניהם אמונה מחוייבת אין שידומה חלופה, וזהו אמרו והתחייבה להם ההגשמה הגמורה, והאמינו בה, ונתן הסבה למה היתה האמונה הזאת הכרחית ומחוייבת לדעתם. ואמר שהתחייב מצאת הפסוק ומצאת המופת, אם מצאת הפסוק לפי שהוא מיחס כלים והוראים גשמיים לבורא ית', וזהו אמרו. וראו שהם אם יפרדו מזאת האמונה יכזיבו הכתוב. ואמנם מצאת המופת כי האנשים האלה חשבו שאחרי שהאל ית' נמצא, יתחייב שיהיה גשם כי אין הנמצא זולת הגשמי, וזהו שאמר הרב וגם ישימו השם נעדר אם לא יהיה גוף, ר"ל שלדעתם ישימו את הש"י נעדר אם לא ישימו גוף: אמנם כו'. לפי שהאנשים האלה נטלו לדעתם באמונה הכוזבת מצאת השכל ומצאת הכתובים, רצה הרב להשיב על שתי ראיותיהם, ואמר שמה שצריך שיאמר בהרחקת הגשמית רצו לומר מצד עצמו

First page of Rambam's *Moreh Nevuchim,* with commentaries

appearance, two Hebrew renditions were made, one by Rabbi Shmuel ibn Tibbon and the other by Rabbi Yehudah al Charizi. Ibn Tibbon's rendition has been accepted as the authoritative one because of its faithfulness in conveying the exact meaning of the author in all its nuances. Ibn Tibbon consulted Rambam through correspondence regarding the meaning or wording of all difficult passages. Rambam himself gave the translation his approbation, calling Ibn Tibbon the most able and fit person to discharge this task. The translation by Al Charizi, although superior as far as beauty of language and elegance of style is concerned, was lacking in precision and exactness of meaning. Rabbi Avraham, Rambam's son, expressed dissatisfaction with Al Charizi's translation because of its inaccuracy.[9]

Influence of Moreh Nevuchim

Interest in this philosophical work was not limited to Jewish scholars but it was assiduously studied by thinkers of the non-Jewish world, both Arabic and non-Arabic. Even in Rambam's lifetime, the book was transcribed into Arabic letters and used extensively by Mohammedan scholars. Not long afterwards, a Latin rendition of the *Guide for the Perplexed* appeared in Europe, followed by Spanish and Italian versions. At about the middle of the nineteenth century, interest in the work by non-Jewish philosophers was revived as a result of a new translation into French by Solomon Munk. Subsequently, it was translated into almost all European languages. The work wielded great influence on the scholastic philosophers of the Middle Ages, and was extensively quoted by many of them. Notably Albertus Magnus, Thomas Aquinas, Duns Scotus and Roger Bacon. Thus, Maimonides occupies a most prominent place in the annals of general theological philosophy.

The *Moreh Nevuchim*, dealing with abstruse metaphysical concepts, became one of the most commented upon philosophical classics of all time. There are more than thirty commentaries on it in Hebrew by known authors, and many more by unknown authors. It is interesting to note that some of these commentaries include explanations from the Kabbalistic perspective. This indicates that beneath the philosophical veneer of the *Moreh Nevuchim* lie Kabbalistic ideas, and by studying it only from the rationalistic-philosophic point of view one does not plumb the depth of its content. This is in accord with the view of those who hold that Rabbi Moshe ben Maimon was not only a Talmudist and philosopher but also a Kabbalist.

During the past 200 years, it has been revealed in Chabad-Lubavitch literature that he was also a mystic steeped in the study and traditions of Kabbalah. In fact, the source of some laws in his Code, *Mishneh Torah,* are found only in Kabbalistic literature.

Rambam, through this monumental work laid the foundation for all subsequent Jewish philosophic inquiry known as *Chakirah,* and stimulated centuries of philosophic Jewish writing. Whether the philosophers accepted his conclusions or not, whether commenting and elaborating on his ideas or criticizing them, each one was influenced to a large degree by his approach and ideas. His writings served as the foundation upon which they continued to build. The *Moreh Nevuchim* has dominated *Chakirah* since its appearance down to the present time and exerted a profound and enduring influence on Jewish thought.

As the fame of the *Moreh Nevuchim* spread, the enthusiastic recognition of the work was countered by vehement opposition on the part of those opposed to the attitudes and principles of philosophy. The struggle between the protagonists of philosophic inquiry and its opponents lasted for decades after the passing of the Rambam, and, unfortunately, at some periods took the form of acrimonious protest and even personal hostility against the intents and character of the holy Rambam.

PHYSICIAN AND MEDICAL AUTHOR

Rambam reached the peak of his professional reputation as a doctor when he was appointed to the staff of the court of Saladin as royal physician. He was charged with personally supervising the health of the Grand Vizier Alfadhel, as well as members of the royal family. He devoted himself wholeheartedly and tirelessly to his profession, and his fame as a conscientious, skilled, compassionate physician radiated far and wide. His reputation spread to such an extent that King Richard the Lionhearted of England sought his medical services and offered him the position as his personal physician. Rambam declined the offer, preferring to remain in Egypt where he had been appointed *Nagid* (Supreme Head) of all Egyptian Jewry, employing his dignified position to protect his co-religionists throughout the Islamic world.

Over fifteen treatises on the theory and practice of medicine have been attributed to him. Among these are a treatise on poisons and their antidotes which was used throughout the Middle Ages, a discourse on asthma, and a list of hygienic regulations which would lead to a healthful life. His rabbinic works, too, are replete with references to medicine and its practice and numerous rules for healthful physical well-being.

Oath for Physicians

There is an ancient physicians oath which articulates the physicians deeply felt obligation to heal the sick. Rambam, as a devoted physician and *guide for the perplexed*, composed an oath for all physicians, Jews and gentiles,* which expresses the profound obligation of the physician to heal with devotion and humility, and a prayer for G-d's assistance and intervention.

The oath attributed to Rambam reads:

O G-d, Thou has formed the body of man with infinite goodness; Thou has united in him innumerable forces incessantly at work like so many instruments so as to preserve in its entirety this beautiful house containing his immortal soul, and these forces act with all the order, concord, and harmony imaginable. But if weakness or violent passion disturb this harmony, these forces act against one another and the body returns to the dust whence it came. Thou sendest then to man Thy messengers, the diseases which announce the approach of danger, and bid him prepare to overcome them. The Eternal Providence has appointed me to watch over the life and health of Thy creatures. May the love of my art actuate me at all times, may neither avarice, or miserliness, nor the thirst for glory or a great reputation engage my mind; for, enemies of truth and philanthropy, they could easily deceive me and make me forgetful of my lofty aim of doing good to Thy children. Endow me with stength of heart and mind, so that both may be ready to serve the rich and the poor, the good and the wicked, friend and enemy, and that I may never see in the patient anything else but a fellow creature in pain.

If physicians more learned than I wish to counsel me,

---

* The Rambam opines (*Mishneh Torah*, Kings 8:10), that it is incumbent upon the Jew to influence the gentile to observe the Seven Noahide Laws, the universal code of morality and ethics given to all mankind, and that this too was instructed to Moses at Sinai.

inspire me with confidence in and obedience toward the recognition of them, for the study of the science is great. It is not given to one alone to see all that others see. May I be moderate in everything except in the knowledge of this science; so far as it is concerned, may I be insatiable; grant me the strength and opportunity always to correct what I have acquired, always to extend its domain; for knowledge is boundless and the spirit of man can also extend infinitely, daily to enrich itself with new acquirements. Today he can discover his errors of yesterday, and tomorrow he may obtain new light on what he thinks himself sure of today.

G-d, Thou hast appointed me to watch over the life and death of Thy creatures: here am I ready for my vocation.

Some, however, question the attribution of this text to Rambam.

Rambam's Demise

The last years of his life were devoted to unceasing work as a physician, to revising and adding to his many writings, to acting as Chief Rabbi of Egypt and spiritual leader of the farflung Jewish communities who sought his sage counsel. The years of weariness took their toll and he suffered from various ailments and weaknesses until on the twentieth of Tevet, in 1204, close to seventy years of age, he passed away. He was mourned by Jewry the world over. In Fostat, both Jews and Moslems publicly mourned him for three days. In Jerusalem, special funeral services were held and a general fast was declared. In the synagogues, the Scriptural passages dealing with the penalties for transgressing G-d's commandments (the *Tochacha*) and the narrative in the Book of Samuel describing the capture of the Ark by the Philistines, which concludes with the verse, "The glory is departed from Israel, for the Ark of

G-d is taken," were read. He was interred in the holy city of
Tiberias, where to this day thousands of Jews come to pray
and meditate upon the life and teachings of this "guide for
the perplexed" of all generations, of whom it is said, "From
Moshe to Moshe, there arose none like Moshe."

A study group in Rambam's *Mishneh Torah* at his tomb in Tiberias.
On the stone is the epitaph "From Moshe to Moshe there arose
none like Moshe"

1. According to some historians, Rambam was born in 1133; according to others, in 1138.

2. R. Maimon wrote a commentary on the Talmud, which his son R. Moshe mentions in his Introduction to the Mishnah and which he used as a source in the preparation of his own work. R. Maimon also composed a code of laws concerning the prayers and the Festivals. All his works were lost in the course of time.

3. See Rambam, Commentary on *Avot* 4:5; Code, *Hilchot Talmud Torah* 3:10.

4. Heb. *Torah she-be-al peh*. The part of the Divine revelation to Moses at Mt. Sinai which is not recorded in the Bible (the Written Law — *Torah she-be-ktav*) but was transmitted by oral tradition.

5. According to some, at the age of thirty-five.

6. According to some, it took him fourteen years to complete the *Mishneh Torah*.

7. An allusion to Deuteronomy 34:12 referring to the mighty hand of Moshe Rabbeinu.

8. A volume of notations of sources was recently published by Kehot Publication Society, Brooklyn, N.Y., 1984.

9. Recently a new, annotated translation into modern and lucid Hebrew was made from the Arabic text by Rabbi Yoseph D. Kappach.

IMPORTANT DATES AND EVENTS
IN THE LIFE OF RAMBAM

1135 (1138)

14th of Nissan, birth of Rabbi Moshe ben Maimon, Rambam, in Cordova, Spain.

1148

The Almohades, a fanatic Moslem sect of Northern Africa, capture Cordova. The Maimon Family flees Cordova and enters an eleven year period of wandering through Southern Spain and Northern Africa.

1158 (1161)

Rambam begins writing his commentary on the Mishnah.

1159

The Maimon family settles in Fez, the capital of Morocco.

1162 (1163)

Rambam composes and disseminates "Iggret HaShmad" (Epistle Concerning Apostacy).

1164 (1165)

The Maimon family leaves Fez and sets out for, and journeys through, the Holy Land.

1166

They leave the Holy Land and settle in Alexandria, Egypt.

1166 ca.

Rabbi Maimon, father of Rambam, passes away.

1165 (1168)

Rambam completes his Commentary on the Mishnah.

1167 (1170)

Rambam begins composing Sefer HaMitzvot and Mishneh Torah.

1169

He writes and sends Iggeret Teiman to the Jews of Yemen.

1171 ca.

Rabbi David, brother of Rambam, drowns in a shipwreck.

1171 ca.

Rambam settles in Fostad, Egypt, where he lives for the rest of his life.

1171 (1174)

End of the Fatimid Caliphate. Saladin becomes king of Egypt.

1177 ca.

Appointed Chief Rabbi by the Jewish community of Cairo.

1177 (1180)

Completes writing Mishneh Torah.

1186

28 of Sivan, his son, Rabbi Avraham, is born.

1186 (1190)

Completes Moreh Nevuchim (Guide for the Perplexed).

1204

Passes away on the 20th of Teves. He was laid to rest in the holy city of Tiberias.

GLOSSARY

Aggadah (Aggadaic): Homiletic and narrative (in contrast to the halachic or legal) Rabbinic teachings found in the Talmud.

Amora, pl. Amoraim: "Expounders." Name given to the Rabbinic teachers in both the Holy Land and Babylonia during the post-Mishnaic period of the Talmud (219-500 c.e.).

Bet Hamikdash: Holy Temple in Jerusalem. The first was built by King Solomon and destroyed by Nebuchadnezzar of Babylon; the second was built by the returning exiles from Babylon and destroyed by Titus of Rome (70 c.e.); the third and everlasting one, will be built by *Mashiach*.

Gaonim (pl. of *Gaon*): (lit., "Excellency"); heads of the Torah academies of Babylon in the post-Talmudic period (589-1038).

Dayan (pl. *dayanim*): Judge in a Jewish court of law.

Gemara: The work based on, and interpreting, the *Mishnah*, which together comprise the Talmud.

Halachot (pl. *Halachah*): Torah laws.

Kaddish: Prayer for the souls of the departed.

Karaism: Post-Talmudic sect rejecting the Oral Tradition of the Torah, accepting only literal and individual interpretations of the written text of the Torah.

Karaites: see *Karaism*.

Mashiach: The Messiah.

Mishnah: The codification of the Oral Tradition of the Torah, by Rabbi *Yehudah HaNassi* (218 c.e.).

Mitzvot (pl. of *mitzvah*): Commandments. There are 613 commandments in the Torah.

Moshe Rabbeinu: (lit., "Moshe our Teacher'"); Moses.

Pilpul: Method of Talmudic study, consisting of examining all arguments pro and con of a given text, often involving reconciliation of apparent contradictory texts.

Pirkei Avot: Tractate of the Mishnah dealing primarily with moral and ethical teachings, popularly known as "Ethics of our Fathers".

Resh Galuta: Exilarch. Head of the Jewish community in Babylon, who had complete political autonomy in directing Jewish affairs. The holders of this office were descendants of the House of King David.

Rif: Acronym for *R*abbi *Y*itzchak (al)*F*asi (Fez), author of "Halachot", one of the most important contributions to Talmudic study after the completion of the Talmud, (1013-1103 c.e.).

Sanhedrin: The Supreme Court in ancient Israel, consisting of 71 members.

Shulchan Aruch: (lit., "prepared table"); the authoritative code of Jewish law, codified by Rabbi Yosef Karo (1488-1575 c.e.).

Yehuda HaNassi, Rabbi: (lit.: "Yehudah the Prince"); known also simply as "Rebbe." Compiler of the *Mishnah*.

Yeyasher Kochacha: (lit., "May your strength be firm"; an expression of approval and thanks.

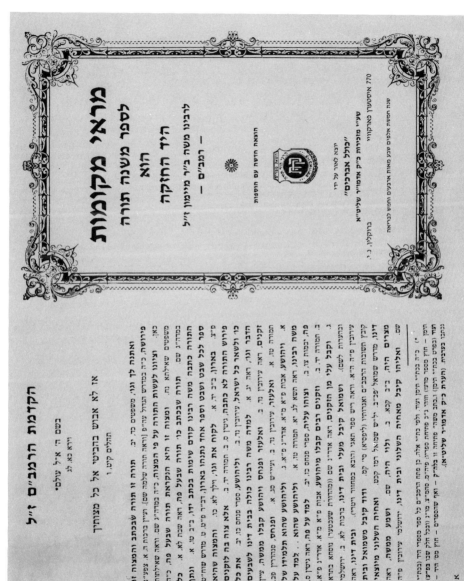

Pages from *Marei Mekomot* — a compilation of sources for the Rambam's *Mishneh Torah*, published by Kehot Publication Society, Brooklyn, 1984